PIANO / VOCAL / GUITAR

CAMILA CABELLO

CAMILA

ISBN 978-1-5400-2433-6

7777 W. BLUEMOUND RD. P.O. BOX 13819 MILWAUKEE, WI 53213

In Australia Contact:
Hal Leonard Australia Pty. Ltd.
4 Lentara Court
Cheltenham, Victoria, 3192 Australia
Email: ausadmin@halleonard.com.au

Visit Hal Leonard Online at
www.halleonard.com

NEVER BE THE SAME

Words and Music by CAMILA CABELLO,
ADAM FEENEY, NOONIE BAO, LEO RAMI
DAWOOD, JACOB LUDWIG OLOFSSON
and SASHA YATCHENKO

Ambient Pop, in 2

ALL THESE YEARS

Words and Music by CAMILA CABELLO,
ADAM FEENEY, KAAN GUNESBERK,
JEFF GITELMAN and MUSTAFA AHMED

Soulful Pop

Your hair's grown a lit - tle long - er,
Could - nt help but o - ver - hear _ you.

your arms look a lit - tle strong - er.
It sounds like you're hap - py with _ her.

Your eyes, just as I _ re - mem - ber.
But does she kiss you like I kissed _ you?

Background vocals maintain 3-part harmony to end.

SHE LOVES CONTROL

Words and Music by CAMILA CABELLO,
ADAM FEENEY, ILSEY JUBER,
LOUIS BELL, SONNY MOORE
and MUSTAFA AHMED

INSIDE OUT

Words and Music by CAMILA CABELLO,
ADAM FEENEY, TYLER WILLIAMS,
KAAN GUNESBERK and BRITTANY HAZZARD

HAVANA

Words and Music by CAMILA CABELLO, LOUIS BELL,
PHARRELL WILLIAMS, ADAM FEENEY, ALI TAMPOSI,
BRIAN LEE, ANDREW WOTMAN, BRITTANY HAZZARD,
JEFFERY LAMAR WILLIAMS and KAAN GUNESBERK

Additional Lyrics

Jeffery.
Just graduated, fresh on campus, mmm.
Fresh out East Atlanta with no manners, damn.
Fresh out East Atlanta.
Bump on her bumper like a traffic jam (jam).
Hey, I was quick to pay that girl like Uncle Sam. (Here you go, ay).
Back it on me, shawty cravin' on me.
Get to diggin' on me (on me).
She waited on me. (Then what?)
Shawty cakin' on me, got the bacon on me. (Wait up.)
This is history in the makin' on me (on me).
Point blank, close range, that be.
If it cost a million, that's me (that's me).
I was gettin' mula, man, they feel me.

CONSEQUENCES

Words and Music by CAMILA CABELLO,
AMY WADGE, EMILY WEISBAND
and NICOLLE GALYON

REAL FRIENDS

Words and Music by CAMILA CABELLO,
ADAM FEENEY, WILLIAM WALSH,
LOUIS BELL and BRIAN LEE

this town.

I just wan-na talk a-bout noth-ing with some-bod-y that means

SOMETHING'S GOTTA GIVE

Words and Music by CAMILA CABELLO,
JESSE ST. JOHN GELLER, ALEX SCHWARTZ,
JOE KHAJADOURIAN, SARAH HUDSON
and JAMES ABRAHART

*Lead vocal written an octave higher than sung.

IN THE DARK

Words and Music by CAMILA CABELLO,
ADAM FEENEY, SIMON WILCOX,
TE WHITI WARBRICK, MADISON LOVE
and JAMES ABRAHART

INTO IT

Words and Music by CAMILA CABELLO,
ADAM FEENEY, LOUIS BELL,
KAAN GUNESBERK, RYAN TEDDER
and JUSTIN TRANTER

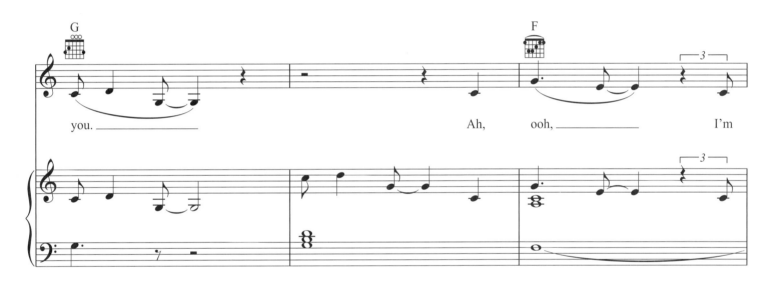

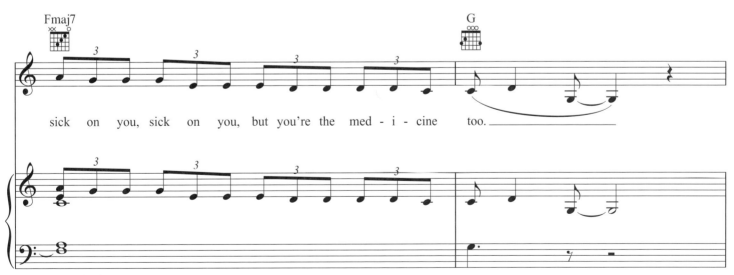

Recorded a half step lower.